Grade 6 Violin
Sight Reading Intensive Exercise

(Based on ABRSM Grade 6
Violin Sight Reading Syllabus)

Regina Pratley

ISBN: 1981292969
ISBN-13: 978-1981292967

DEDICATION

Dedicated to all the students that are going to take the ABRSM grade 6 violin exam.
Wishing you all the best in the exam! ☺

CONTENTS

Sunshine in the Morning

Andate espressivo

1

Hope

Andantino

2

The Playground

A Rainy Day

Tragedy

Cotton Clouds

Andante espressvio

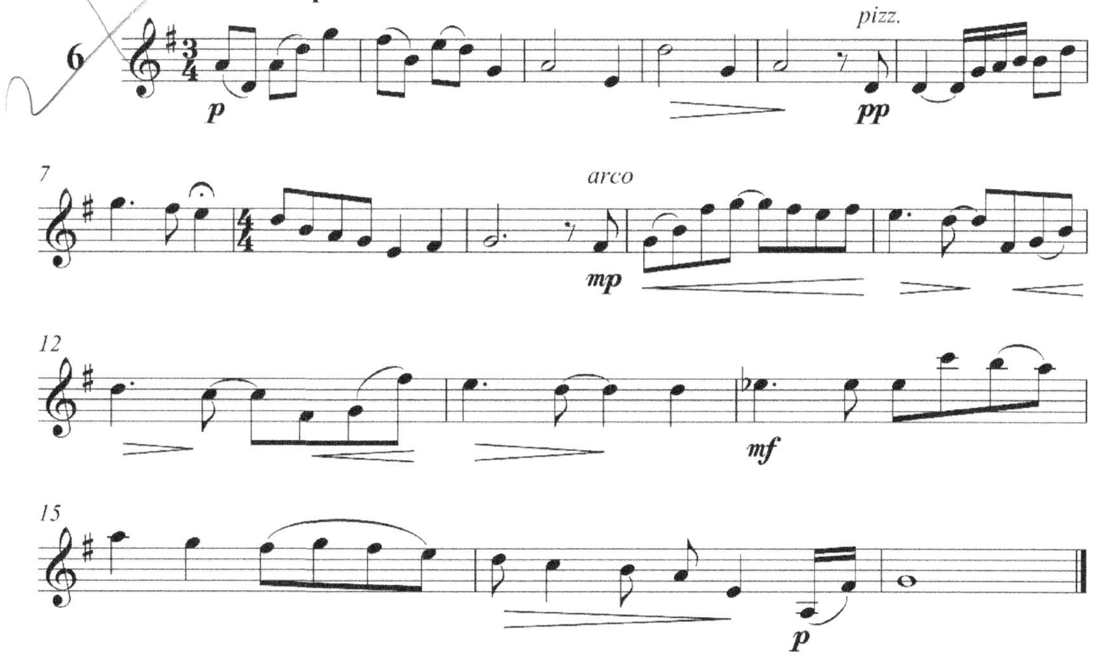

The Picnic Day

Allegro

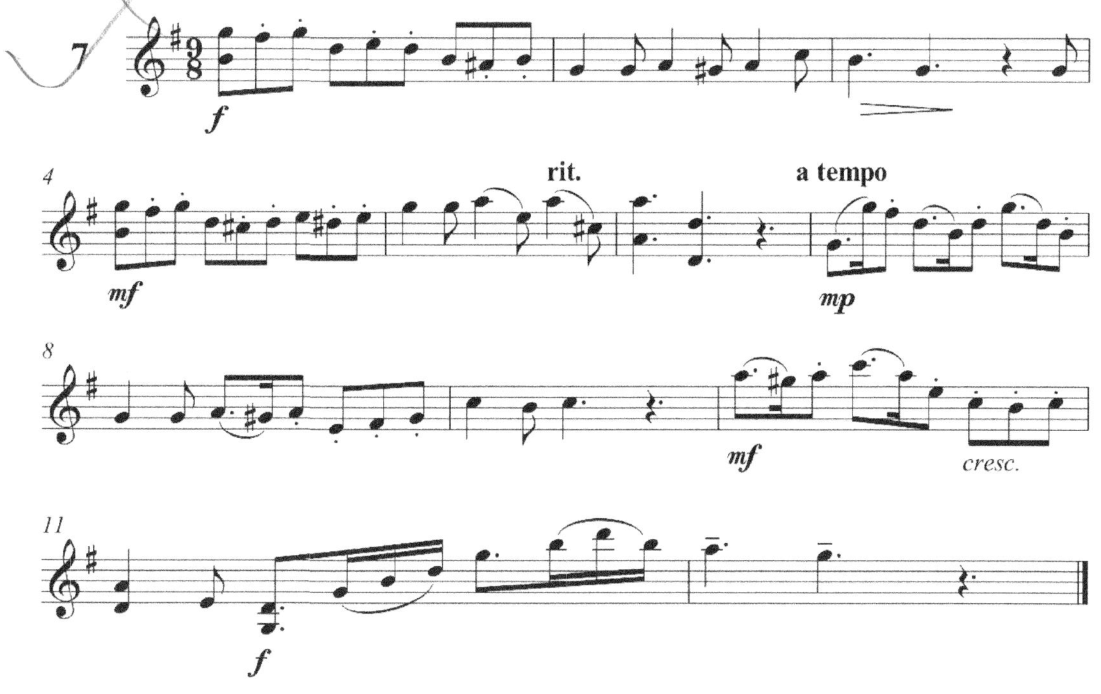

Capriccio

Sighs

A Phantom

A Sweet Day

Andante cantabile

Birthday Party

Scherzando

Destiny

Doloroso

A Road Without Light

Fearfully

Elegy

Butterfly

A Forgotten Dream

A Sad Autumn

18

A Summer Night

19

Snowy Evening

The Merry Go Round

Thanksgiving Day

Dancing

Night Train

Once Upon a Time...

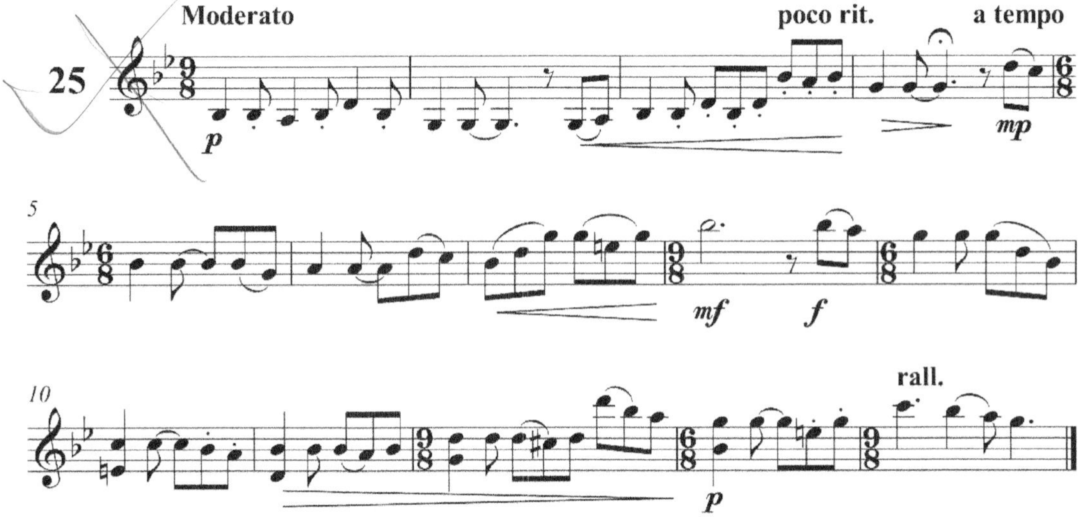

Coffee Time

The Dream House

The Naughty Cousin

Remembering

Grasp the Dream

Sunday

Lullaby

Sleepwalking

Andante

33

Stormy Sea

Agitato

34

Foggy

Wishes

Andante espressivo

On the Beach

Allegretto con brio

An Old Music Box

Secret Love

The Clown

Con moto

40

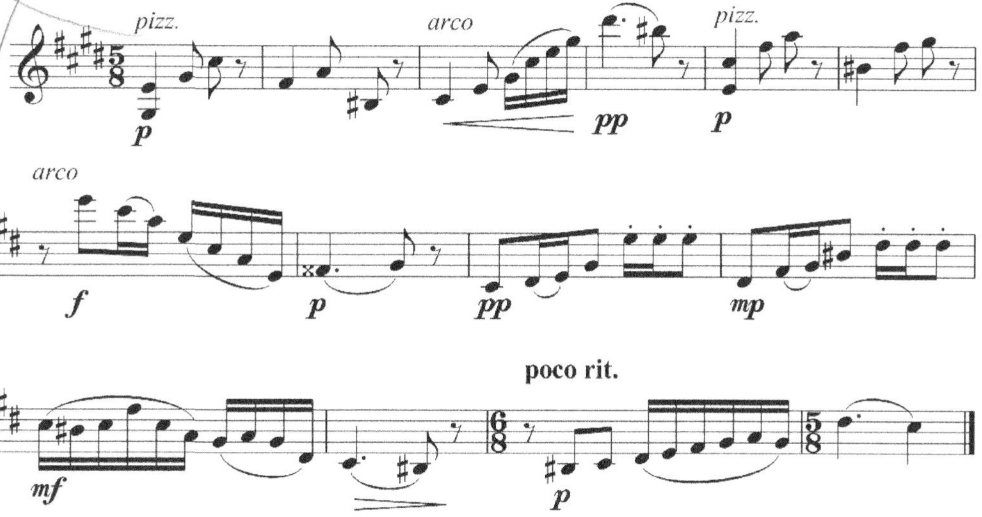

A Present for Julia

Andante cantabile

The Magician

Allegro giocoso

A Boat Trip

Andantino

At the Theatre

Allegretto

Free As the Bird

Notes

Printed in Great Britain
by Amazon